EXPLORING COUNTRIES

Japan

PAMELA McDOWELL

MEDIA ENHANCED BOOKS
AV2 BY WEIGL
ADDED VALUE • AUDIO VISUAL

www.av2books.com

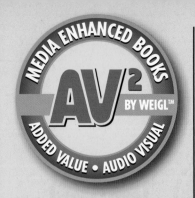

AV² provides enriched content that supplements and complements this book. Weigl's AV² books strive to create inspired learning and engage young minds in a total learning experience.

Your AV² Media Enhanced books come alive with...

Audio
Listen to sections of the book read aloud.

Key Words
Study vocabulary, and complete a matching word activity.

Go to **www.av2books.com**, and enter this book's unique code.

Video
Watch informative video clips.

Quizzes
Test your knowledge.

BOOK CODE

Q 7 4 9 1 5

Embedded Weblinks
Gain additional information for research.

Slide Show
View images and captions, and prepare a presentation.

AV² by Weigl brings you media enhanced books that support active learning.

Try This!
Complete activities and hands-on experiments.

... and much, much more!

Published by AV² by Weigl
350 5ᵗʰ Avenue, 59ᵗʰ Floor
New York, NY 10118
Websites: www.av2books.com   www.weigl.com

Library of Congress Cataloging-in-Publication Data

McDowell, Pamela.
 Japan / Pamela McDowell.
     pages cm. — (Exploring countries)
 Includes index.
 ISBN 978-1-4896-1018-8 (hardcover : alk. paper) — ISBN 978-1-4896-1019-5 (softcover : alk. paper) —
ISBN 978-1-4896-1020-1 (single user ebk.) — ISBN 978-1-4896-1021-8 (multi user ebk.)
 1. Japan—Juvenile literature. I. Title.
 DS806.M228 2014
 952—dc23
                              2014005943

Printed in the United States of America in North Mankato, Minnesota
1 2 3 4 5 6 7 8 9 0 18 17 16 15 14

042014
WEP150314

Project Coordinator Heather Kissock
Art Director Terry Paulhus

Photo Credits
Every reasonable effort has been made to trace ownership and to obtain permission to reprint copyright material. The publishers would be pleased to have any errors or omissions brought to their attention so that they may be corrected in subsequent printings.

Weigl acknowledges Getty Images as its primary image supplier for this title.

Contents

Japan Overview

Japan is located off the east coast of the continent of Asia. This mountainous country includes four large islands and more than 3,000 smaller islands. Most residents live in cities on the coast of the main island, Honshu. The Japanese have always depended on the sea to provide food, a means of transportation, and protection. They respect cultural traditions as well as modern advances. Today, Japan is a global leader in technology and manufacturing, with the world's fourth-largest **economy**.

Many people enjoy skiing and snowboarding in the Japanese Alps, a group of three mountain ranges on Honshu.

The Shinkansen, or bullet train, is a symbol of Japan's state-of-the-art technology.

つばめ
TSUBAME
KYUSHU SHINKANSEN TSUBAME 800 SINCE 2004

A traditional Japanese robe is called a kimono.

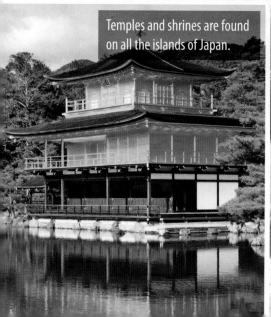

Temples and shrines are found on all the islands of Japan.

The ancient sport of sumo wrestling remains popular today.

Exploring Japan

Japan is an **archipelago** that stretches for about 1,500 miles (2,400 kilometers) in the western Pacific Ocean. The country's four main islands are Hokkaido, Honshu, Shikoku, and Kyushu. Japan's total area covers 145,914 square miles (377, 915 sq. km). That is slightly smaller than the state of California.

Japan does not share any land borders with other countries. Its closest neighbors lie to the west, across the Sea of Japan. These countries are South Korea, North Korea, and Russia. To the south of Japan is the East China Sea, and to the east lies the Pacific Ocean.

China

North Korea

Sea of Japan

South Korea

N

East China Sea

Mount Fuji

Map Legend

- Japan
- Land
- Water
- Lake Biwa
- Kanto Plain
- ▲ Mount Fuji
- Capital City

SCALE

500 Miles

500 Kilometers

Mount Fuji

Mount Fuji, or Fuji-san, is the highest mountain in Japan. It is 12,388 feet (3,776 meters) tall. The mountain and area around it are part of Fuji-Hakone-Izu National Park.

Russia

Lake Biwa

Kanto Plain

Kanto Plain

Tokyo

Pacific
Ocean

Tokyo

Lake Biwa

Lake Biwa is Japan's largest lake. Located on the island of Honshu, it covers 259 square miles (670 sq. km). Parts of the lake are almost 340 feet (105 m) deep.

Tokyo

Tokyo is the capital city of Japan. It is also the world's largest **urban** area. Tokyo is the country's center for government, business, and culture.

Kanto Plain

The Kanto Plain is the largest lowland area in Japan. Three river systems flow from the surrounding mountains through the Kanto Plain to the Pacific Ocean. More people live in this area than any other part of Japan.

LAND AND CLIMATE

Japan is located in an area where three of Earth's **tectonic plates** meet below the Pacific Ocean. That is why volcanoes and earthquakes are so common in Japan. Over the past 2.6 million years, volcanoes and the forces produced by moving plates helped create the Japanese islands.

There are about 200 volcanoes in Japan. Of these, 60 are active. This means they have erupted in the fairly recent past and are likely to erupt again. About 1,000 **tremors** and several strong earthquakes shake Japan each year. Powerful earthquakes near Japan sometimes cause **tsunamis**.

In 2011, a strong earthquake in the Pacific Ocean caused a tsunami. Waves destroyed coastal communities in Japan, and more than 15,000 people were killed.

The islands of Japan stretch north to south. Most parts of the country have a **temperate** climate. In the north, Hokkaido and other, smaller islands have cooler temperatures and long cold winters. In the center of the country, the other three large islands have warmer weather with more rain. In the far south, the tiny island of Okinawa has a **subtropical** climate, with heavy rainfall all year. In March, it is possible to play on the beach in Okinawa and ski in Hokkaido.

Mountains have a big effect on Japan's climate. The Japanese Alps cause the interior region of Honshu to be very wet. The mountain areas may get more than 160 inches (400 centimeters) of rain a year. In the winter, heavy clouds move across the Sea of Japan, bringing rain or snow to the west coast and mountains. The air that continues to the east coast is much drier. Eastern Hokkaido receives only 36 inches (91 cm) of rain each year.

In the summer, the winds are reversed. Warm air passes over the Pacific Ocean to the east coast of Japan. It is wetter on the east coast during the summer. Sometimes, winds from the Pacific bring violent storms called typhoons.

Land and Climate BY THE NUMBERS

1707 Year Mount Fuji, an active volcano, last erupted.

80% Portion of Japan's land that is mountainous.

33 Feet
Height of one of the largest waves that hit Japan during the 2011 tsunami. (10 m)

3 Average number of typhoons that hit Japan's main islands each year.

Kabira Bay Beach on Ishigaki Island near Okinawa is known for its white sand and clear blue water.

PLANTS AND ANIMALS

A variety of plants grow on Japan's islands. Spruce and fir trees are common on Hokkaido and in the mountains of Honshu. Maple, oak, and katsura trees also grow in these colder regions. In the highest mountains of Hokkaido, there are small shrubs and pines.

Deciduous forests cover the mountains of Shikoku and Kyushu. Evergreen trees and fan palms grow in low-lying areas. Ferns cover the forest floor. Pine trees grow on the sandy dunes on the coast of the southern islands.

Japan is home to more than 150 species, or kinds, of **mammals**. They include Japanese flying squirrels, Ezo brown bears, and Amami hares. Small populations of leopard cats live on the island of Iriomote. More than 600 species of birds can be found living in or **migrating** through Japan during the year.

The warm and cold ocean currents that flow around the islands bring a variety of sea life. Whales, dolphins, and porpoises are common. They share the waters with salmon, sardines, tuna, crabs, and oysters.

Japanese macaques, sometimes called snow monkeys, live farther north than any other monkey in the world.

NATURAL RESOURCES

Japan has few natural resources. Much of the country is covered with forests, but many forested areas are mountainous. This makes it difficult to harvest the wood. Gold, silver, lead, and zinc have been found in the country, but not in large amounts. Japanese companies must **import** these and other raw materials, which are then used to make finished products for sale in Japan or other countries.

Much of Japan's land is not suitable for farming. The country must import a great deal of food for its people. The largest farms are on Hokkaido. Farmers there grow rice in **paddies** and raise dairy and beef cattle. The fish in the oceans around Japan are another valuable source of food.

Japan imports coal and oil to meet much of its energy needs. Since the 1970s, the country has built more than 50 nuclear power plants to produce electricity. The 2011 tsunami caused major damage to the Fukushima Daiichi plant. The disaster led the Japanese government to study the risks of nuclear power and make stricter safety standards a priority.

Natural Resources BY THE NUMBERS

Almost 30%
Portion of Japan's electricity provided by nuclear power plants before the tsunami in 2011.

5.3 Million Number of tons of seafood caught by Japanese fishers in 2013. (4.8 million tonnes)

68% Portion of Japan that is forested.

Rice paddies are often flooded naturally by rivers and rainfall. Sometimes, rice farmers use pipes or ditches to bring in water.

TOURISM

People visit Japan for the country's natural beauty, as well as to enjoy both ancient and modern cultural attractions. Historic shrines, temples, and churches are popular with tourists. In 2013, for the first time, Japan had more than 10 million foreign visitors.

Visitors can enter the hollow Great Buddha of Kamakura statue.

Many tourists spend time in the city of Tokyo, visiting old and new landmarks. Shoppers find the newest electronics and high fashion, too. The Imperial Palace is the home of the **emperor** and his family. Part of the palace's garden is open to visitors each day. Sensoji Temple, built in 645 AD, is the oldest Buddhist temple in Tokyo. Outside the temple, stalls sell souvenirs and snacks. The city's newest and tallest landmark is the Tokyo Skytree, which opened in 2012. This observation and communication tower is 2,080 feet (634 m) tall.

Japan has several ancient castles. Himeji Castle in southern Honshu houses a collection of traditional swords called *katana*.

South of Tokyo is Kotokuin Temple and its grounds, where the Great Buddha of Kamakura stands. This bronze statue, formed from hot metal in 1252, is more than 43 feet (13 m) tall. Kinkakuji is a Buddhist temple in Kyoto. Kinkakuji, which means "Temple of the Golden Pavilion," was built for the **shogun** Ashikaga Yoshimitsu in 1397. Part of the building is covered in gold leaf.

Japan's 30 national parks feature seacoasts and forests. Skiing, hiking, and scuba diving attract visitors looking for adventure. About 200,000 people climb Mount Fuji every year. It takes three to eight hours to make the climb, depending on weather and crowds. Jigokudani Monkey Park is another natural area. This park lies in the mountains of Honshu, near the city of Nagano. Visitors come here to see the Japanese macaques.

Today, tourists from around the world visit the Peace Memorial in Hiroshima. The Genbaku Dome was the only building to survive the atomic bomb dropped on the city in 1945, near the end of World War II.

Tourism BY THE NUMBERS

17 Number of **UNESCO** World Heritage Sites in Japan.

3 MILLION Number of people who go through Shinjuku Station in Tokyo each day, making it the world's busiest train station.

1983 Year that the Tokyo Disney Resort opened.

2001 Year that Universal Studios opened a theme park in Osaka.

33% Portion of Mount Fuji climbers each year who are not Japanese.

INDUSTRY

About one-fourth of Japan's workers are employed in manufacturing industries. Japan is one of the world's largest producers of motor vehicles, electronic equipment, machinery, and **textiles**. Automakers Toyota, Nissan, and Honda have customers worldwide. Sony and Panasonic make electronics products used in homes, businesses, and factories in many countries. The world's largest video-game company is Nintendo, headquartered in Kyoto.

Japan has become a world leader in railway technology. The Shinkansen moves people around the country at high speeds. In 2013, a new model called the N700A was built. Controls can brake or slow the train automatically during changes in terrain or to avoid hitting another train.

Many Japanese people work in steel mills, oil refineries, and shipyards along the northwest shore of Tokyo Bay. These industries are located near deep-water ports, where raw materials come into the country. There is no space inland for industry to expand, so coastal areas of Tokyo Bay have been filled in to create new land.

60% Portion of the world's top-ten largest vehicle manufacturers located in Japan.

1878 Year the Tokyo Stock Exchange, now one of the world's largest stock markets, first opened.

2014
Year that Japan was banned from whaling in the Antarctic.

The Japanese corporation Fuji Heavy Industries produces cars in Ota.

GOODS AND SERVICES

MORE THAN $770 BILLION
Total value of the goods Japan exports each year.

18% Portion of Japan's exports that are sold to China.

About 10%
Portion of the land in Japan that can be farmed.

After World War II, Japan focused on industrial growth. Workers in all types of manufacturing were needed. Japan became a leader in producing and **exporting** goods using new technologies. The growth of Japan's economy was based to a large extent on selling these goods to customers in the United States and Europe. More recently, China, South Korea, and countries in Southeast Asia have become major customers for Japanese exports. Japanese companies have also moved some of their factories out of Japan to Asian countries where workers earn less money.

Today, more than two-thirds of Japanese workers are employed in the service industry. Workers in this industry provide a service instead of producing goods. They include people who work in advertising, tourism, education, government, and health care.

Communications is another industry that has grown quickly in Japan. There are hundreds of radio and television stations. Four-fifths of people in Japan use the internet.

Agriculture contributes a small amount to Japan's economy. Fewer than 4 percent of Japanese workers are employed in agriculture. Japan grows as much rice as it needs. Other main crops include vegetables and fruit.

Many Japanese restaurants serve sushi, which is raw or cooked vegetables and seafood wrapped in rice and seaweed.

INDIGENOUS PEOPLES

The **indigenous** people of Japan are called the Ainu. Scientists believe the Ainu are **descendants** of the Jomon people. The Jomon traveled to Japan from Siberia and other areas in northeastern Asia about 30,000 years ago.

The Jomon lived in pit dwellings, a type of home in which the floor is several feet (meters) below the level of the ground. Pieces of Jomon pottery have been found on all four main islands of Japan. The Jomon relied on hunting, fishing, and gathering plants to feed themselves.

Like the Jomon, the Ainu hunted bears and deer in the winter. They used arrows and spears dipped in a poison made from the roots and stalks of certain flowers. In the summer, the Ainu fished for salmon, gathered plants, and grew crops. They made clothing from tree bark.

The Ainu developed their own language, religion, and customs. Traditionally, men grow beards, and women tattoo their lips, hands, and arms. About 25,000 Ainu live in Japan today. Often, they have lighter skin and hair colors than most Japanese.

For many years, **prejudice** against the Ainu was common. More recently, programs have been started to preserve and teach the Ainu language and culture. The Japanese government officially recognized the Ainu as an indigenous people in 2008.

Today, some Ainu wear a traditional robe with bold designs during special ceremonies. The cloth is made from the fibers of an elm tree native to Hokkaido.

Indigenous Peoples BY THE NUMBERS

13th Century
Period when Ainu culture, as it is known today, was established.

3 Number of windows in a traditional Ainu home.

1994 Year the first Ainu was elected to the national government.

EARLY SETTLERS

Waves of **immigrants** began arriving in Japan from southern Asia around 400 BC. They settled in Kyushu and spread to Honshu. These people, called the Yayoi, were skilled toolmakers and weavers. They used bronze and iron to make tools, weapons, and objects such as bells.

The Yayoi brought rice with them from other parts of Asia. They settled on low-lying plains where this grain would grow well. Different groups, or clans, of Yayoi came to control different areas. Present-day Japanese are descendants of the Yayoi people.

As the Japanese population grew and spread over all the main islands, the Ainu were pushed out of many areas where they had lived. Contact with the Japanese also brought diseases that killed many Ainu. Others were taken from their villages and forced to work for the Japanese.

Over time, the remaining Ainu people moved north. They traveled to Hokkaido and the smaller Kuril Islands, which are now controlled by Russia. Small Ainu villages developed near rivers and along the coast of Hokkaido.

The Ainu people had no written language. History and folklore was passed down through stories told by the older village members.

Early Settlers BY THE NUMBERS

1884
Year that a major discovery of Yayoi pottery was made near Tokyo.

About 100
Number of Yayoi clans in today's Japan by the first century AD.

More Than 10,000
Number of Ainu objects on display at the Nibutani Ainu Cultural Museum.

THE AGE OF EXPLORATION

The bodies of water around Japan protected it from invasion by foreigners. Kublai Khan, the 13th-century leader of the Yuan **Dynasty** in China and Mongolia, tried and failed twice to invade Japan. During this time, the shoguns and **samurai** were powerful rulers, allowing few people to enter or leave Japan.

Japan's first contact with the Western world was in 1543, when several Portuguese sailors were shipwrecked and landed on Kyushu. The local military leaders, who had not seen guns before, were interested in the sailors' firearms. Soon, Portuguese traders were making voyages to Japan. They brought guns and silver, and they returned home with silk.

Dejima was an artificial island built in 1636 for Portuguese traders. It later became a Dutch trading post. Today, a miniature model of Dejima stands in Nagasaki.

Missionaries were the next to arrive. A Spanish priest named Francis Xavier brought **Christianity** to Japan in 1549. Other priests soon followed. In the 1600s, a few Dutch, Chinese, and Korean merchants were allowed to use one port to trade with Japan. However, the shoguns grew suspicious of the outsiders. Christianity was banned in the 1630s, and all foreigners were forced to leave. Japanese people were forbidden to travel beyond the islands, and the country was closed for two centuries.

Samurai followed a code that valued courage, loyalty, and honor.

In 1853, U.S. naval leader Matthew Perry sailed four ships into Tokyo Bay. Perry demanded that Japan trade with the United States. After Japanese leaders refused, Perry returned the following year with a larger, more powerful fleet. Japanese leaders knew that Western countries were strong, and they were fearful of the guns on Perry's ships. They signed an agreement in 1854 to trade with the United States and to protect any stranded sailors.

Centuries of shogun rule over Japan came to an end in the 1860s, and the country's emperor became its most powerful leader. This period of change in government control is often called the Meiji Restoration. It is named for Emperor Meiji, who came to power in 1867. Under Meiji, Japan began to build railroads, factories, banks, and schools. Japanese leaders used the West as a model for developing their country.

Just two decades after Matthew Perry's arrival in Japan, paintings showed the Yokohama waterfront with foreign ships and steam locomotives. Japan's isolation and its lack of Western technology had come to an end.

The Age of Exploration BY THE NUMBERS

1,600 Number of sailors on the seven ships Perry brought to Japan in 1854.

150,000
Number of Christians in Japan 50 years after the first missionaries arrived.

Almost 700 Years
Length of time that shoguns were the most powerful leaders in Japan.

POPULATION

Japan's first **census** was taken in 1920. At that time, 57 million people lived in the country. In 2013, the population was more than 127 million. Japan is the tenth most-populated country in the world.

Japan is a crowded country. On average, there are more than 900 people per square mile (350 per sq. km). That is 10 times the figure for the United States.

More than 90 percent of Japan's population lives in cities and the suburban areas around them. Even in farming and fishing villages in the countryside, some residents commute to urban centers for work. Tokyo, formerly named Edo, is Japan's largest city.

In 2013, more than 37 million people lived in the greater Tokyo area, or GTA. The GTA includes the region within 30 miles (50 km) of the center of the city. Today, 12 cities in Japan have more than one million people. The cities of Osaka-Kobe, Nagoya, and Fukuoka-Kitakyushu each have more than 2.8 million residents.

Although Japan's population grew rapidly in the past, it is no longer increasing. Often, families do not have a large number of children. It is estimated that the country's population will decline by about 20 million people by the year 2050.

Almost 30 percent of Japan's total population lives in and around Tokyo.

Population BY THE NUMBERS

25%
Portion of Japan's population that is age 65 or older.

80.9 Number of years that a Japanese man can expect to live.

87.7 Number of years that a Japanese woman can expect to live.

99% Portion of Japanese people age 15 or older who can read.

POLITICS AND GOVERNMENT

In the late 1800s and early 1900s, Japan built up its armed forces and used its military power to gain control of other areas. Japan took over Korea in 1910. It attacked and overpowered large areas of China in the 1930s. In the early 1940s, at the beginning of World War II, Japanese forces conquered Southeast Asia and took control of many islands in the western Pacific.

Japan attacked the U.S. Navy base at Pearl Harbor, Hawai'i, on December 7, 1941. The United States and other countries fought against and defeated Japan in World War II. The United States dropped two atomic bombs, on the cities of Hiroshima and Nagasaki, to force Japan to surrender in 1945.

Japan adopted a new, postwar **constitution** in 1947. It established a parliamentary system of government and outlawed war. The national parliament, or legislature, is called the Diet. It is made up of two houses. The House of Representatives, called the lower house, has 480 seats. The House of Councillors, or upper house, has 242 seats. Both houses must pass a bill in order for it to become law.

The head of the government is the prime minister, who is chosen by the Diet. Japan still has an emperor. However, the emperor has no political power.

Under Japan's constitution, the House of Representatives has more power than the upper house during disagreements about legislation.

Politics and Government BY THE NUMBERS

1989
Year that Akihito became emperor of Japan.

15 Number of judges on the Supreme Court, Japan's highest court.

47 The number of prefectures, or local government regions, in Japan.

1868 Year that Tokyo became the capital of Japan.

CULTURAL GROUPS

About 98 percent of the population is Japanese. Other cultural groups include Chinese and Koreans. Starting in 1910, Korean laborers moved, or were sometimes forced to move, to Japan for work. Most Chinese immigrants or people of Chinese descent live in Japan's major port cities.

The Japanese character called kokoro can mean "heart," "mind," or "spirit."

China had a strong influence on Japan's language and religions in the fourth and fifth centuries AD. Early Japanese literature was influenced by China as well. Language and religious practices slowly changed during the time that the shoguns kept Japan isolated from the rest of the world.

Japanese writing uses characters called *kanji* that came from China about 1,900 years ago. Most Japanese know only about 4,000 out of 60,000 kanji. Books and newspapers use only 1,850 kanji. Japanese is written from top to bottom beginning at the right-hand side of the page.

An important part of Japanese culture is the tea ceremony, which is also called the Way of Tea. It involves several special steps to serve guests.

Different **dialects** of Japanese are spoken throughout the country. One explanation for the large number of dialects is Japan's geography. In the past, the country's many mountains and islands separated groups of people from one another. People in different areas developed their own versions of the language. Starting in 1886, students in Japan have learned the same written language. Today, the dialect in Tokyo has become the national standard used in television and radio.

The two main religions in Japan are Shintoism and Buddhism. Most Japanese follow both. About 84 percent of the population is Shinto, and 71 percent is Buddhist. The Shinto religion respects nature and the past. Gods and goddesses live in water, animals, plants, and the Sun. Buddhism focuses on ancestors and **reincarnation**. Funerals in Japan often are performed in the Buddhist tradition. Weddings are usually Shinto.

As part of a traditional Shinto wedding, priests lead the bride, groom, and family members in a procession.

ARTS AND ENTERTAINMENT

The Japanese respect their traditional arts. Many forms of Japanese theater remain popular. Kabuki, which developed out of the older classical Noh theater, features costumed performers and music. Kyogen is Japan's traditional comic theater. Bunraku, Japanese puppet theater, uses large wooden puppets operated by human performers onstage. Singers offstage provide music.

> Noh is one of the oldest existing forms of theater, dating from the 14th century.

Traditional arts include **calligraphy**, a type of flower arranging called ikebana, and silk weaving. For hundreds of years, musicians have played stringed instruments such as the banjo-like shamisen. These instruments often are used in traditional forms of theater.

Western culture also influences entertainment and the arts in Japan. Movies, television programs, and music from North America and Europe are popular, especially with young people. At the same time, Japanese forms of entertainment, such as karaoke, have spread around the world. The word *karaoke* means "empty orchestra." Karaoke, invented in Tokyo in the late 1970s, is the use of a device that allows people to sing along with recorded music of all kinds.

> The koto is a traditional Japanese musical instrument with 13 strings.

Manga, or Japanese comic books, have become popular in many countries. There are different kinds of manga, including western, science fiction, and romance. They are enjoyed by people of all ages. The story is told in a series, with a new book published each week. A manga series can have sales of up to 5 million copies weekly in Japan. In fact, 40 percent of printed material in Japan is manga.

The Japanese animation style called animé was developed in the 1960s. Animé characters that have become well-known worldwide include Sailor Moon and Hello Kitty. The popular *Dragon Ball Z* video series led to the production of movies and video games based on the characters. Miyazaki Hayao's animé film *Spirited Away* received an Academy Award for best animated film in 2003.

Arts and Entertainment BY THE NUMBERS

11th Century
When Murasaki Shikibu wrote the world's first novel, *The Tale of Genji*.

More Than 50 Million
Total number of albums sold by Ayumi Hamasaki.

---

3 Number of people needed to operate a Bunraku puppet.

TWO Number of Nobel Prizes for Literature awarded to Japanese writers. The award was given to Yasunari Kawabata in 1968 and Kenzaburo Oe in 1994.

Popular singer Ayumi Hamasaki, or Ayu, first appeared on Japan's music charts in 1995. She is sometimes called the Empress of Pop.

SPORTS

Baseball, introduced to Japan in the 1870s, is now a popular sport. Two professional leagues started in the 1950s. Each league has six teams, and the league winners meet in the Japan Series for the championship. Sadaharu Oh played for the Tokyo Yomiuri Giants from 1959 to 1980. He hit a record 868 home runs. Other baseball stars, such as Daisuke Matsuzaka, Ichiro Suzuki, and Koji Uehara, have played for Major League Baseball teams in the United States.

Soccer has increased in popularity in Japan. The women's national team won the International Federation of Association Football (FIFA) Women's World Cup in 2011 and the silver medal at the 2012 Olympic Games. There are youth soccer leagues and two dozen professional teams in Japan.

Outfielder Ichiro Suzuki was born in Kasugai in 1973. He moved to the United States to play Major League Baseball in 2001.

In 2011, Japan became the first Asian nation to win the World Cup.

Sumo wrestling dates back to the eighth century. Sumo tournaments were a way to give thanks for the harvest. Ancient rituals are still part of modern events. Wrestlers, called *rikishi*, knot their hair as ancient warriors did and wear a special silk belt. Matches take place in a ring called a *dohyo* that has a clay floor covered with sand. Wrestlers fight until one leaves the ring or touches the ground with any part of his body other than the soles of the feet.

The traditions of the samurai are preserved in the **martial arts**. Kendo is a form of fencing. Karate, **jujitsu**, and **aikido** are all popular. Japanese athletes have won many Olympic medals in **judo**.

In 2012, Japan sent 295 athletes to the Summer Olympics in London, England. They returned with 38 medals, the highest number the country had ever won. Tokyo will host the Summer Olympics in 2020.

Sports BY THE NUMBERS

140
Number of games played by professional baseball teams in Japan each season.

8
Number of medals won by Japanese athletes at the 2014 Winter Olympic Games in Sochi, Russia.

440 POUNDS
Weight of some sumo wrestlers. (200 kilograms)

Yuzuru Hanyu won the gold medal in men's figure skating at the 2014 Winter Olympic Games. It was Japan's first ever gold in the event.

Mapping Japan

We use many tools to interpret maps and to understand the locations of features such as cities, states, lakes, and rivers. The map below has many tools to help interpret information on the map of Japan.

Map of Japan

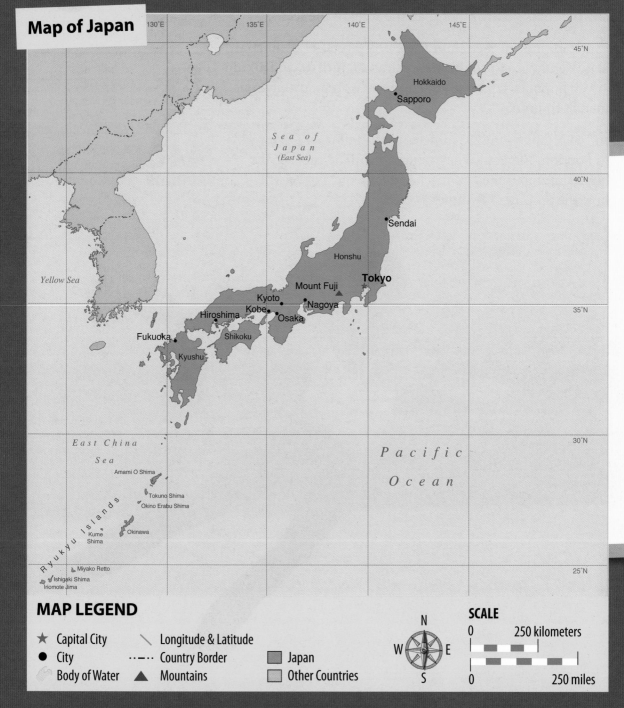

MAP LEGEND

★ Capital City
● City
🌊 Body of Water
╲ Longitude & Latitude
·-·-· Country Border
▲ Mountains
▨ Japan
▨ Other Countries

SCALE
0 ___ 250 kilometers
0 ___ 250 miles

N W E S

Mapping Tools

- The compass rose shows north, south, east, and west. The points in between represent northeast, northwest, southeast, and southwest.
- The map scale shows that the distances on a map represent much longer distances in real life. If you measure the distance between objects on a map, you can use the map scale to calculate the actual distance in miles or kilometers between those two points.

- The lines of latitude and longitude are long lines that appear on maps. The lines of latitude run east to west and measure how far north or south of the equator a place is located. The lines of longitude run north to south and measure how far east or west of the Prime Meridian a place is located. A location on a map can be found by using two numbers where latitude and longitude meet. This number is called a coordinate and is written using degrees and direction. For example, the city of Tokyo would be found at 36°N and 140°E on a map.

Map It!

Using the map and the appropriate tools, complete the activities below.

Locating with latitude and longitude

1. What mountain is found at 35°N and 139°E?
2. What island is found at 26°N and 128°E?
3. What body of water is found at 40°N and 135°E?

Distances between points

4. Using the map scale and a ruler, calculate the distance between Sapporo and Sendai.
5. Using the map scale and a ruler, calculate the approximate length of the island of Honshu.
6. Using the map scale and a ruler, calculate the approximate distance between Kyoto and Tokyo.

Quiz Time

Test your knowledge of Japan by answering these questions.

1 What countries are Japan's closest neighbors?

2 How many active volcanoes are there in Japan?

3 When was the last time Mount Fuji erupted?

4 What is another name for Japanese macaques?

5 Which industry employs the most workers?

6 What is the name of Japan's main indigenous people?

7 How many cities in Japan have more than one million residents?

8 What is the name of Japan's parliament?

9 What are the two main religions in Japan?

10 What is the name of the ring in which sumo matches take place?

ANSWERS

1. South Korea, North Korea, and Russia
2. 60
3. 1707
4. Snow monkeys
5. Service industry
6. Ainu
7. 12
8. Diet
9. Shintoism and Buddhism
10. *Dohyo*

Key Words

aikido: a form of self-defense that forces opponents to lose their balance
archipelago: a group of islands
calligraphy: decorative handwriting
census: an official count of people living in an area
Christianity: a religion based on the teachings of Jesus Christ
constitution: a written document stating a country's basic principles and laws
deciduous: losing leaves at the end of the growing season
descendants: people who share common ancestors
dialects: the ways that a language is spoken in an area
dynasty: a succession of rulers from the same family
economy: the wealth and resources of a country or area
emperor: the male ruler of an empire, which is a group of nations or territories headed by a single leader

exporting: sending goods to another country for sale
immigrants: people who move to a new country or area to live
import: to bring in from another country
indigenous: native to a particular area
judo: a sport based on jujitsu
jujitsu: the art of self-defense using holds, throws, and blows
mammals: animals that have hair or fur and that drink milk from the mother
martial arts: Asian arts of combat and self-defense practiced as a sport
migrating: moving from one place to another at different times of year
missionaries: people who travel to another country or area to spread their religious faith
paddies: wet land where rice is grown
prejudice: an unfair feeling of dislike for a person or group because of race, sex, religion, etc.

reincarnation: rebirth of the soul in another body
samurai: an ancient Japanese warrior
shogun: an ancient military ruler of Japan
subtropical: relating to fairly high temperatures and rainfall throughout the year
tectonic plates: sections of Earth's surface that move very slowly
temperate: not very hot or very cold
textiles: woven or knit cloths
tremors: small earthquakes
tsunamis: large destructive waves caused by underwater earthquakes or volcanoes
UNESCO: the United Nations Educational, Scientific, and Cultural Organization, whose main goals are to promote world peace and eliminate poverty through education, science, and culture
urban: relating to or located in a city

Index

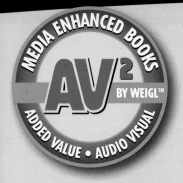

Log on to www.av2books.com

AV² by Weigl brings you media enhanced books that support active learning. Go to www.av2books.com, and enter the special code found on page 2 of this book. You will gain access to enriched and enhanced content that supplements and complements this book. Content includes video, audio, weblinks, quizzes, a slide show, and activities.

AV² Online Navigation

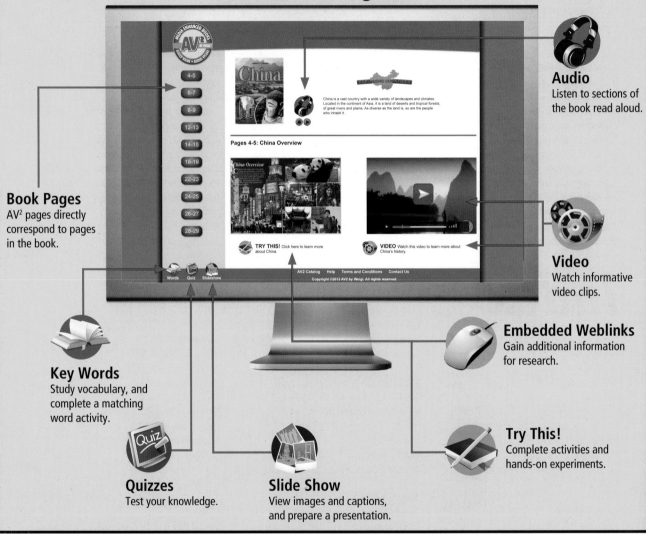

Audio
Listen to sections of the book read aloud.

Book Pages
AV² pages directly correspond to pages in the book.

Video
Watch informative video clips.

Key Words
Study vocabulary, and complete a matching word activity.

Embedded Weblinks
Gain additional information for research.

Try This!
Complete activities and hands-on experiments.

Quizzes
Test your knowledge.

Slide Show
View images and captions, and prepare a presentation.

AV² was built to bridge the gap between print and digital. We encourage you to tell us what you like and what you want to see in the future.

Sign up to be an AV² Ambassador at www.av2books.com/ambassador.

Due to the dynamic nature of the Internet, some of the URLs and activities provided as part of AV² by Weigl may have changed or ceased to exist. AV² by Weigl accepts no responsibility for any such changes. All media enhanced books are regularly monitored to update addresses and sites in a timely manner. Contact AV² by Weigl at 1-866-649-3445 or av2books@weigl.com with any questions, comments, or feedback.